·I am· CONFIDENT

I am HEALTHY

I am loved

I am
SMART

-I am- VERY SPECIAL

I AM STRONG

SUPER POWER

I am loved

I matter

Be Kind to yourself

I am a QUEEN

I am Smart

GIRL POWER +

BLessed

I AM SO GRATEFUL

I AM BRAVE

I AM THAT GIRL

I am confident

I AM CAPABLE ENOUGH

I am HAPPY

i am successful

i'm FEELING good

I AM STRONG!

I AM LOVED

I am Proud of You

TODAY -I am- THANKFUL

PROMISE

TODAY
-I am-
THANKFUL

I am
Special

I am
a limited
edition

love

I ♥

LOVe

fAmILy

THANK
YOU

CREATE

Yes I Can!

I CAN
DO IT

PET

MY

My birthday Queen

DO IT

HAPPY BIRTHDAY

Let's eat CAKE!

It's My Birthday

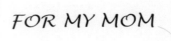

FOR MY MOM

Best.
Mom.
Ever.

MY DAD IS MY HERO

I ♥ My DAD

BEST DAD

MY

BROTHER

IS THE BEST

SISTER
LOVE

VACATION

HOLIDAY

SEASIDE

SNOW

SCHOOL

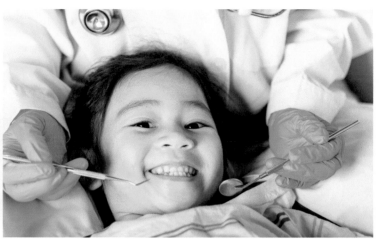

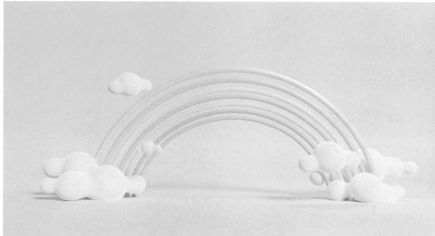

MY

GIRL
ROOM

Thank you

for choosing our Vision Board Clip Art Book

As a special GIFT I am offering you a complimentary guide to download.

This guide will explore practical strategies to teach values to your kids, focusing on setting goals for kids, fostering good behavior, helping them understand feelings, introducing morality basics, and more.

Open the camera on your phone
(as if you're going to take a photo)
Hold the phone on the QR CODE below then
a link will appear on your screen
Tap on the link to get your FREE GUIDE

GET FREE GUIDE

Guide for Parents
TEACHING VALUES TO KIDS

Much Love
Leen

Made in United States
Troutdale, OR
01/01/2025